Donation 5/16/08

YOUNG OBSERVER
VAMPIRE BATS
and other creatures of the night

Philip Steele

Kingfisher

NEW YORK

KINGFISHER
Larousse Kingfisher Chambers Inc.
95 Madison Avenue
New York, New York 10016

First edition 1995
10 9 8 7 6 5 4 3
Text copyright © Larousse plc 1995
Illustrations copyright © Larousse
plc 1995
Design copyright © David West
Children's Books 1995

LIBRARY OF CONGRESS CATALOGING-IN-PUBLICATION DATA
Steele, Philip
Vampire bats and other creatures
of the night / Philip Steele.—
1st American ed.
p. cm.—(Young observer)
Includes bibliograhical references
(p.) and index.
1. Nocturnal animals—Miscellanea
—Juvenile literature. [1. Nocturnal
animals—Miscellanea.] I. Title.
II. Series.
QL755.5.S88 1995
591.51—dc20 95-6105 CIP AC

ISBN 1-85697-575-4

Printed in Hong Kong

Conceived and created by

David West • CHILDREN'S BOOKS

Consultant: Michael Chinery
Cover illustration: Rebecca Hardy
 and Rob Shone
Illustrations: Mike Atkinson (Garden
 Studio) 4tl,tr,b, 5, 6bl, 7tr,b, 10,
 11tr & m, 12br, 20, 21m & b,
 22–23, 24–25, 28–29, 30–31,
 32–33, 34–35, 36–37; Roger Kent
 (Garden Studio) 4ml, 6tr, 11bl, 12tr
 & bl, 19tr; Harry Smith (Garden
 Studio) 7m, 12tl, 18, 19l; Myke
 Taylor (Garden Studio) 8–9,
 16–17, 26–27; Josephine Martin
 (Garden Studio) 14–15
Line illustrations: Rob Shone

CONTENTS

INTRODUCTION
3

CHAPTER ONE
Living in the Dark 4
The Young Observer Quiz 13

CHAPTER TWO
Phantoms of the Night Sky 14
The Young Observer Quiz 21

CHAPTER THREE
Deep in the Shadows 22
The Young Observer Quiz 31

QUIZ ANSWERS
32

USEFUL WORDS
38

INDEX
40

INTRODUCTION

Nocturnal animals are mysterious because we see them so rarely. What *is* that scrabbling outside the window? Are those strange, flashing lights eyes? Is that a raccoon looking for a late-night snack? Or is it a bloodsucking vampire bat? What *does* sneak into your house under the cover of darkness . . . ?

As darkness falls, most wild animals are returning home—but the creatures of the night are just starting to wake up. Owls, moths, and bats are only the beginning. Meet the many amazing animals that spend their lives in a world of twilight and shadow, and find out what they do there.

There are dozens of fascinating facts in this book. You can test what you've read—and some of what you may already know—with the Young Observer trivia quiz at the end of each chapter. If you get stuck, the answers are in the back.

CHAPTER ONE

LIVING IN THE DARK

When we are snuggling up in bed at night, many wild creatures are just waking up. We rarely see them in the darkness, but we often hear them. Owls hoot eerily in the woods, and foxes bark in yards.

Just why do some animals prefer to live by night? Where do they hide away during the daytime? And how do they find their way around in the darkness?

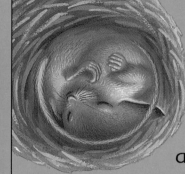

THE HARVEST MOUSE (*left*) avoids sharp-eyed falcons and other daytime *predators* by staying asleep in its nest. But at night it has a lot of other enemies—cats, foxes, badgers, and owls all like to munch on a juicy mouse!

THE EUROPEAN BADGER (*below*) spends the day dozing in an underground lair called a sett. It lumbers out at dusk in search of its supper. On the menu are worms, grubs, and baby rabbits, as well as mice.

CAMOUFLAGE protects some animals during the daytime. Their body coloring and shape help them to blend into the background, so they don't need to creep away into holes and burrows. They can stay right where they are instead. Geckos are nocturnal lizards that live in warm countries. The leaf-tailed gecko of Indonesia (*above right*) spends its days hiding on tree trunks. So does the buff-tip moth (*right*)—it looks just like a broken twig.

BIG PREDATORS such as lions don't have to hide—no other animal dares to attack them! These big African cats like to hunt at night, when it's cooler. They mostly laze around during the heat of the day, sleeping in the shade.

Most crabs live in the sea, but robber crabs live on land around the Indian and Pacific oceans. They hide from predators by day, emerging at night to feed on fallen fruit.

Dwarf puff adder

THE DWARF PUFF ADDER is another animal that avoids the daytime heat. It lives in the African deserts and escapes from the hot sun by burrowing into the sand.

SOME PLANTS, such as honeysuckle and evening primrose, give out their sweet perfume mainly by night. This attracts long-tongued moths that sip at the sugary *nectar*. By feeding after dark, moths avoid hungry birds and do not have to compete with day-flying insects. Dormice (*right*) sleep by day, but will scamper through tangled honeysuckle stems after dark, greedily nibbling at buds, young shoots, and bark.

Elephant hawkmoth

A HUNGRY KIT FOX bounds after a young jackrabbit, as night falls on the deserts of the West. Many animals have become night hunters because their *prey* is nocturnal. Others hunt after dark because a sleeping animal is an easy target!

Kit fox

Jackrabbit

WHY DO SLIMY SLUGS feed at night? The toadstools, leaves, and stems that they eat are there during the day, but hot sunshine would dry out the slugs' bodies and kill them. Slugs, wood lice, and many other minibeasts like dark, moist conditions because their tiny bodies need to be kept damp.

The tuatara lives on islands off the New Zealand coast. During the nesting season it shares its burrow with seabirds. It spends the day there and hunts at night for insects.

Red slug

DARK, WET NIGHTS are also ideal for frogs and other *amphibians* such as newts and salamanders. These animals have lungs for breathing in life-giving *oxygen* from the air, but they also take in oxygen through their skin. Amphibians have to keep their skin moist so that they can do this. On the wettest nights, even eels, which are fish, can travel overland.

Freshwater eel

Common frog

Long-tailed salamander

NOISY NEIGHBORS

can keep you awake at night! Who or what is doing all that hooting and howling?

Insects can make a lot of noise on warm summer evenings. Male crickets are busy trying to attract mates. They make their shrill chirruping noise by rubbing the base of their wings together.

CROAKING AND BOOMING

noises mean that it is spring, and male frogs or toads are gathering at their breeding grounds and calling for mates. They make the noise by pumping air into special pouches on their throats. Females soon respond and come hopping or crawling to the pond— but they stay quiet!

Gray tree frog

HOWLING AT THE MOON is a chilling

sound—it means that wolves or other wild dogs are close by. Despite their fierce reputation, wolves do not attack humans unless provoked. They howl to "talk" to members of the pack or to warn rivals off their **territory**.

WHOO, HOO-HOO, WHOO, WHOO!

Owl calls are eerie—people once thought the sounds came from evil spirits! The calls made by different **species** vary greatly. Some owls shriek, while others hoot, moan, or wail. The calls warn other owls to keep away from the bird's hunting ground.

Tawny owl

The nightingale sings by night and day, but is best heard after dusk, when other birds sleep. Its rich and beautiful song is marked by warbles, trills, and whistles. Nightingales are rarely seen because they like to nest in thick scrub.

HOWLER MONKEYS (*below*) live in the South American **rain forests** and take their name from the loud, roaring noises with which they greet the dawn. The monkeys live in groups of up to 45, and each troop produces a deafening chorus that can be heard as far as 3 miles (5km) away! The leading male leads the "singing," with the aim of warning other monkeys away from the troop's feeding grounds.

Long-eared bat

Using sound to find things is called echolocation. It involves measuring the time taken for sounds to travel to an object, and then bounce off it and return—or echo. Bats and some whales use it. A bat's huge ears help it to pick up the echoes.

Reflected echo

High-pitched sound given out

FINDING THE WAY isn't easy in total darkness. Many bats use *echolocation* to avoid bumping into things and to seek out their prey. The long-eared bat may have a pea-sized brain, but its superb sound equipment can register an insect almost instantly.

SOME ANIMALS' EYES are designed for night-hunting. During the day, a cat's pupils are narrow slits.

Spectacled owl

They open after dark, to let in as much light as possible. Cats' eyes have a special lining that reflects light, making their night-sight even better. Some owls' vision is 100 times better than ours because of their big eyes!

MIGRATING **BIRDS** fly through the night, but during the day they have stops to refuel, eating to regain their strength. How do they find their way across the land and oceans in the dark? Scientists think they use the stars to navigate. Some birds may even tune in to the Earth's *magnetic field*.

SHARP HEARING helps night animals to track down prey and listen out for enemies. The little fennec fox lives in the Sahara and hunts in the cool of the night. Its huge ears help it to pick up the slightest sound—and to hunt juicy spiders, scorpions, lizards, and snakes.

Fennec fox

SOME SNAKES hunt in total darkness by sensing the body heat given out by their prey. Most boas and pythons, and many vipers, have tiny pits in their heads that lead to heat-sensitive *cells*. The cells detect even the tiniest temperature change.

Pit opening

Sometimes deadly pit vipers slide into a home as they hunt for a meal. Finding a cozy spot, they curl up for a nap. People can wake up to a nasty surprise!

A SNAKE'S FLICKERING, forked tongue helps it to hunt. Many snakes have poor eyesight and hearing, but they can all sense and track their prey by tasting the air, water, or ground.

A MOTH'S FEATHERY antennae are its nose and its fingers. Each antenna contains thousands of microscopically tiny sense cells that help the moth to smell out a meal or a mate. In some moth species, the males are so sensitive to the females' scent that they can search out a mate from over a mile away.

Antenna

A COCKROACH'S QUIVERING antennae also help it to feel and taste its way. This insect (*below*) scuttles around after dark, hunting for food scraps and dead animals to feast on.

Kiwis are flightless birds that live in New Zealand pine forests. The kiwi's nostrils are at the tip of its bill, and it spends the night probing the forest floor, sniffing out worms, insects, or fruit. It probably also uses the bristles around its bill to help it feel its way around in the darkness.

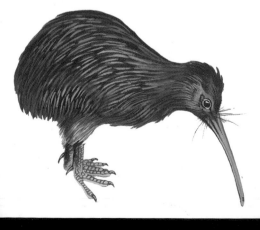

The **Young Observer** *Quiz*

1. Where would you find a Jacobson's organ?

Is it in:

a) A flea's ear?

b) A snake's mouth?

c) A bat's wing?

5. Which animal makes electricity to help it navigate?

Is it:

a) A glowworm?

b) An electric knife fish?

2. Which animal leaves a silvery trail?

Is it:

a) A snail?

b) A slug?

c) A cockroach?

6. Which night animals send messages by drumming?

Is it:

a) Kiwis?

b) Cats?

c) Gerbils?

3. Where can you find rods and cones?

Are they:

a) On the highway?

b) In an eye?

c) In an ear?

7. Where are a cricket's ears?

Are they in:

a) Its head?

b) Its body?

c) Its legs?

4. Who hangs upside down in dark caves?

Is it:

a) Cockroaches?

b) Moths?

c) Bats?

d) Bears?

8. What is a Tasmanian devil?

Is it:

a) A cartoon?

b) An Australian marsupial?

c) An African bat?

ANSWERS ON PAGES 32–33

CHAPTER TWO

PHANTOMS OF THE NIGHT SKY

All kinds of creature take to the wing as dusk falls, fluttering and swooping their way through the night.

What secrets do birds, beetles, bats, and moths hide in the darkness? Why are some bats called vampires, and do they really suck blood? How do owls fly silently? And why do moths fly to certain death in a candle's flame?

OILBIRDS (*above*) are cave dwellers that live in the forests of South America and the island of Trinidad. Their days are spent in complete darkness. At night, they stream out in search of the oily palm fruits on which they like to feed. Unlike most birds, they have a good sense of smell and are guided by the fruits' scent.

GHOSTLY AND WHITE-FACED, a barn owl (*below*) looms out of the twilight on silent wings, to pounce on a mouse. The owl hunts voles and rats, too, and can hear even the slightest squeak made by its prey. These creatures receive little warning of their fate, however—the owl's soft, fluffy feathers muffle the sound of its wingbeats, making its flight virtually noiseless. Like other owls, barn owls gobble their prey whole or tear it up for their chicks. The bones and fur are coughed up once in a while, squashed into dark, cylindrical pellets.

A BROKEN BRANCH may turn out to be nothing of the kind in an Australian forest! It could be a well-camouflaged tawny frogmouth (*right*), waiting for nightfall. This bird's gaping mouth snatches up beetles, grubs, scorpions, lizards, and, from time to time, a mouse.

One of the world's rarest night birds is a New Zealand species of parrot called the kakapo. It can climb trees and glide back to the ground, but it can't fly. It has a strange booming call, and it feeds on wild berries and nectar.

THE BIGGEST GATHERINGS of *mammals* on Earth can be seen in the big cave systems of the southern United States. Mexican free-tailed bats (*left*) can live in colonies numbering up to 30 million. People visit each evening to watch the bats streaming out from their roosts like great clouds of smoke. About 300 bats leave one cave *every* second!

Indian flying fox

BLOODSUCKING is the specialty of the vampire bats of Central and South America (*below*). The bats are only hand-sized, 2 to 4 inches (6 to 10cm) long, but their victims are much larger. Vampires usually attack horses, goats, and cows, but sometimes they nibble the toes of sleeping humans! The bats have razor-edged teeth, and the *saliva* in their mouths makes a victim's blood flow without clotting.

The terrifying, cloaked figure of the human vampire Count Dracula first appeared in 1897 in a horror story made up by the Irish writer Bram Stoker. In Stoker's novel, the bloodsucking Count Dracula is able to change into all sorts of animals, including a bat and a wolf.

FRUIT BATS live in *tropical* countries, where they feed on flower blossoms, nectar, and juicy fruits, such as bananas and guavas. Flying foxes (*left*) are large fruit bats with furry, foxlike faces. Their outspread wings can measure as much as 6 feet (1.8m) across.

MEET THE SMALLEST mammal in the world —and one of the rarest. The wingspan of the tiny creature (*above right*) is smaller than that of some butterflies! Called Kitti's hog-nosed bat, it lives in Thailand and was only discovered in 1973.

THE FISHING BAT (*left*) of Central and South America skims across the surface of seas, lakes, and rivers at night. It trails its long hind legs through the water, using its sharp claws to grasp and hook fish. Fishing bats use echolocation to track their prey—they pick up any ripples or splashes made by a fish breaking the surface of the water.

LIGHT BULBS AND CANDLES attract moths and other night-flying insects. Scientists often use artificial lights to lure insects into traps so that they can be studied. Some moths use the Moon as a kind of compass to keep them on course. If they become confused by another large light, the mistake can be fatal—the moth may burn its wings as it flutters around a hot bulb or flame.

DEATH'S-HEAD HAWKMOTHS (*left*) take their spooky name from the distinctive marking on their backs—it looks just like a human skull. The moths migrate between Europe and Africa. Despite their name, they are harmless, but they do squeak loudly if handled or attacked!

Not all moths are nocturnal, and some cannot even fly. Male vaporer moths have wings and can fly, but the females (right) are wingless and look a bit like spiders. Being wingless makes females an easy target for predators.

The wings of the tropical moon moths can measure up to 5 inches (12cm) across.

CAN MOTHS ESCAPE from a swooping bat? Some species have eardrum-like structures on their bodies that are sensitive to the echolocation squeaks of a bat. To evade its hungry predator, the moth may then loop or power dive like a fighter plane. Another tactic is for the moth to plummet to the ground and hide until it can escape.

THE BEAUTIFUL WINGS of some moths are patterned with big eyelike patches. Moon moths (*left*) have four spots that look just like the iris and pupil in the center of an eye. The eyespots aren't just for decoration, though. When the moth flashes its wings, the spots can startle predators into giving it time to escape.

Inside Mexican jumping beans are tiny grubs that have grown from a moth's eggs. The grubs wriggle around if they get too hot, making the beans bounce up and down too!

LARGE EYES help moths to see at night, just as they do other animals. Unlike our eyes, which have just one lens, insects' eyes have hundreds of tiny, lenslike structures.

GLOWWORMS (*left*) are not worms, but beetles—they have legs, for a start! The male glowworm flies through the night sky, searching for a mate. The female does not have wings, so she cannot fly up to meet him. Instead, she glows to attract him down to earth. She can also switch her greenish-yellow light on and off at will.

TINY FIREFLIES (*below*) can swarm in the thousands at night, each one glowing like the spark from a campfire. Fireflies are small beetles, too. Both males and females have wings, and they flash signals to each other. Most are tropical, but there are some North American and European species.

Animals are not the only living things to make their own light. Some **fungi** *glow in the dark and are visible from as far as 130 feet (40m) away. These toadstools can be seen in forests on the Indonesian island of Sumatra.*

The **Young Observer** Quiz

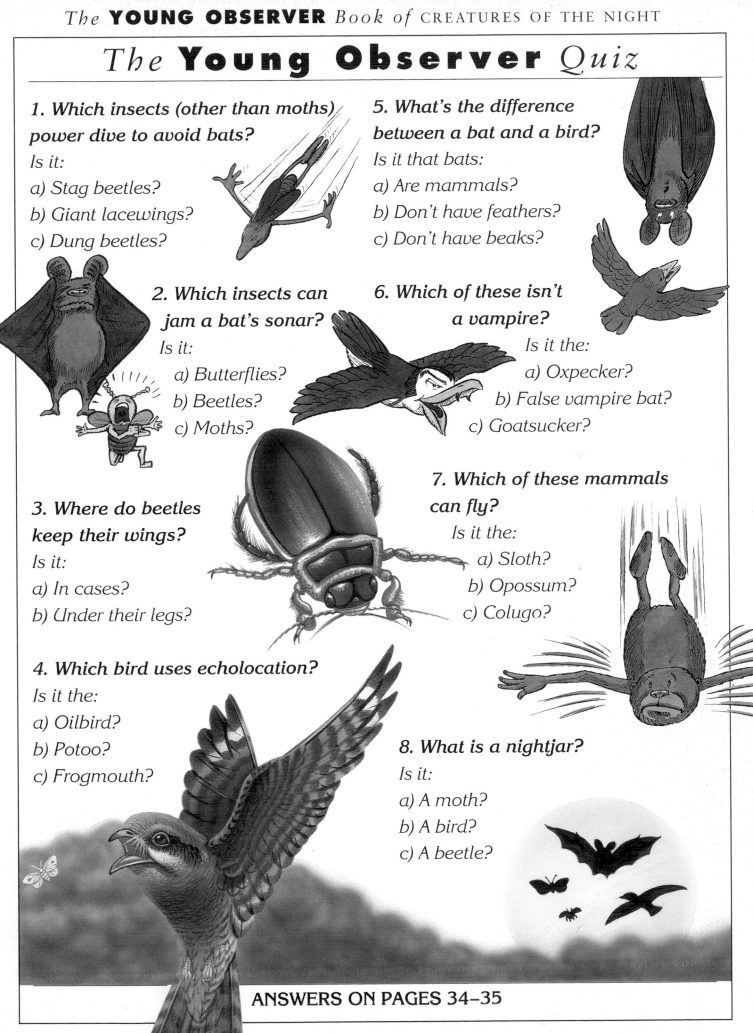

1. Which insects (other than moths) power dive to avoid bats?

Is it:

a) Stag beetles?

b) Giant lacewings?

c) Dung beetles?

2. Which insects can jam a bat's sonar?

Is it:

a) Butterflies?

b) Beetles?

c) Moths?

3. Where do beetles keep their wings?

Is it:

a) In cases?

b) Under their legs?

4. Which bird uses echolocation?

Is it the:

a) Oilbird?

b) Potoo?

c) Frogmouth?

5. What's the difference between a bat and a bird?

Is it that bats:

a) Are mammals?

b) Don't have feathers?

c) Don't have beaks?

6. Which of these isn't a vampire?

Is it the:

a) Oxpecker?

b) False vampire bat?

c) Goatsucker?

7. Which of these mammals can fly?

Is it the:

a) Sloth?

b) Opossum?

c) Colugo?

8. What is a nightjar?

Is it:

a) A moth?

b) A bird?

c) A beetle?

ANSWERS ON PAGES 34–35

CHAPTER THREE

DEEP IN THE SHADOWS

The oceans are home to strange creatures that never see the light of the Sun. Mysterious animals also lurk in rain forests and other wild places.

Otters haunt the riverbank, hunting for a tasty fish or even a small bird, while toads croak by moonlit breeding ponds. Shadowy creatures flit through city parks and yards, too, and some even creep into houses....

Flying fish

THE OCEANS are home to billions of minute plants and animals known as **plankton**. As the Sun sets, the animal plankton rise toward the surface to feed on the plants. Small fish follow this feast, hunted in turn by larger fish.

Squid are jet-propelled, squirting through the water at speeds of up to 30 miles (50km) per hour. Chased by hungry tuna, they sometimes break the surface and fly through the air— they've even been found on boat decks in the morning.

SOME JELLYFISH (*below*) bob to the surface at night and float into shallower waters. Many small sea creatures feed after dark—they are less easy to spot then, and there are fewer hungry predators around.

SOME BIRDS take advantage of the food-rich, nighttime waters. Albatrosses (*right*) and most storm petrels (*below*) are active by day and night. Storm petrels patter across the water on dancing feet, scooping animal plankton and small fish into their beaks. These birds follow boats for the food churned up in their wake. In stormy weather they are sometimes dazzled and confused by the boats' lights and crash onto their decks.

Wilson's storm petrel

Flashlight fish

IS THE WATER ON FIRE? No, the glittering light comes from tiny plant plankton that flash as they are churned up by a passing boat. Other creatures add to the light show, as they rise to feed near the surface at night. Flashlight fish can blink the lights beneath their eyes on and off—they seem to flash more quickly to warn of danger to the school. The lantern fish's rows of twinkling lights are thought to help schools stay together

Lantern fish

MARSHES and other watery places teem with wildlife at night. Because they are home to fish and moisture-loving amphibians, they also attract predators. Night herons (*left*) stand motionless in the darkness before stabbing downward with their long, sharp beaks.

Common European toad

ON WARM NIGHTS IN SPRING, toads wake up from their long **hibernation** and travel to their breeding ponds. They may have to crawl a mile or more. After mating, the female lays long strands of spawn. The eggs will hatch into wriggling tadpoles.

American bullfrogs can grow to 8 inches (20cm) long and leap as high as an adult's head. They have big mouths and big appetites, and can even gulp down mice, birds, and young terrapins. They also have a colossal croak!

The otter's webbed feet help it to swim.

OTTERS ARE SHY creatures that prefer to hunt along riverbanks after dark. They are fantastic swimmers, with webbed feet, waterproof fur, and long, sleek bodies. At night they slip out of their burrows to catch fish, crayfish, and frogs, as well as small mammals and birds.

Hippopotamuses spend most of the hot African day swimming or wallowing in rivers and lakes. In the cool of the night, however, whole familes come ashore to munch on tasty grasses. One animal can eat about 150 pounds (70kg) per day!

MINK are related to otters and have similar lifestyles—and tastes! They are bolder, though, and will even enter a barnyard to attack chickens. They will swim after prey, even though their fur isn't waterproof.

Mink

Blue catfish

CATFISH (*above*) have long whiskers called barbels. These are lined with cells that detect frogs and other food in murky river water and mud. Sea trout (*below*) often swim by night. They grow up in rivers and streams and then swim out to the oceans. They return later to breed and eventually die in their birthplace.

Sea trout

Ocelot

Mouse lemur

Golden potto

Slow loris

EYES BURN IN THE NIGHT

as fierce animals go on the prowl in the rain forest. Shadowy in the daytime, rain forests are darker and even more mysterious at night.

BIG CATS sometimes hunt by day as well as night, but darkness offers the best chance of catching prey. The beautiful ocelot and margay live in the tropical forests of Central and South America, preying on birds and small mammals. The powerful tiger of Asia stalks deer, pigs, and monkeys after dark. Its striped coat gives it good camouflage in the undergrowth.

Tiger

Margay

Lesser bush baby

Tree pangolin

Owl monkey

Tarsier

TREES OFFER SAFETY to many animals, although snakes and climbing leopards are still a danger for some. Many tree-dwelling mammals are nocturnal. The tree pangolin of Africa eats mainly ants, licking them up with its long, sticky tongue. Its body is protected by a coat of horny scales. Rain forest trees are also home to the bush babies and pottos of Africa, and to the lorises of southern Asia. These animals have big, round eyes for seeing in the dark.

THE BIGGEST EYES of any small, nocturnal mammal belong to the tarsiers of Southeast Asia. Their vision is even better because they can swivel their heads to look behind them. As they leap from tree to tree, tarsiers are hunted by owls.

The tamandua is a tree-climbing anteater that feeds by night in the rain forests of Central and South America. It tears apart ant and termite colonies with its sharp claws, then pokes in its snout and gobbles up the insects with its long, sticky tongue. The tamandua is also fond of the honeycombs made by wild bees.

YARDS IN TOWNS AND CITIES also come alive after dark. Animals are attracted by the warmth given off from houses, by scraps of food and other refuse, and by the lack of predators. As towns have spread across the wilderness, many creatures have become used to living closer to humans.

Mouse

EVEN BADGERS (*below*) will enter suburban yards when no people are around. Like many nocturnal animals, they are at risk from road traffic. Many are dazzled by headlights and run over.

CUNNING FOXES (*right*) have always raided barnyards and chicken sheds. Moving into towns, they may kill ducks in the park, search for slugs and beetles in yards, or even raid garbage cans.

American badger

MASKED BANDITS are nighttime visitors to many North American yards. Raccoons (*below*) eat more or less anything—from insects, frogs, crayfish, and mice, to kitchen scraps. They are not at all shy, and will even beg for food.

Hyenas live in Africa and Asia and usually feed on dead animals. Sometimes, though, they visit town garbage dumps under cover of darkness. They have been known to crush bottles—their mouths are so tough that even broken glass does little damage!

HEDGEHOGS (*below left*) snuffle through European gardens and parks after dark. These small, prickly animals eat caterpillars, slugs, and many other garden pests.

WHEREVER THERE ARE PEOPLE, there are rats (*below*) and mice. Garbage and food scraps attract them to alleyways and kitchens at night. Cats are also on the prowl, hunting mice and searching garbage cans.

MINIBEASTS LOVE THE DARK, and the outdoors is crawling with spiders, wood lice, slugs, and snails (*left*) at night. Earthworms come to the surface and pull leaves down into their tunnels to nibble on. Insects such as crane flies flutter into houses through open windows, attracted by the light and warmth.

Beware! Scorpions live in hot places and are mostly nocturnal. Some species have a sting in their tails that can kill you within minutes!

Wood louse

MOLES LIVE UNDERGROUND, but they sometimes dig their way to the surface as they search for worms. Shrews munch on minibeasts by day and by night—they run the risk of starving if they stop eating for longer than an hour.

Mole

Crane fly

Wolf spider

Shrew

The **Young Observer** Quiz

1. What is the owl monkey's other name?

Is it the:

a) Douroucouli?

b) Marmoset?

2. What do numbats and wombats have in common?

Is it that:

a) They're both bats?

b) They're both marsupials?

c) They both eat termites?

3. Which nocturnal animal were the ancient Romans particularly fond of?

Was it the:

a) Edible dormouse?

b) Field mouse?

c) Hamster?

4. Which fish can breathe out of water?

Is it the:

a) Walking catfish?

b) Flying fish?

c) Lantern fish?

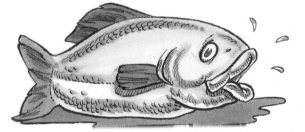

5. Which nocturnal animal uses its middle finger like a fork?

Is it the:

a) Raccoon?

b) Golden potto?

c) Aye-aye?

6. Which animal builds dams?

Is it the:

a) Mudskipper?

b) Mudpuppy?

c) Beaver?

7. Which marsupial sleeps in a tree all day long?

Is it the:

a) Tree shrew?

b) Tree kangaroo?

c) Treecreeper?

8. How did the deathwatch beetle get its name?

Is it because:

a) It eats dead animals?

b) It is said to warn of a death in the house?

c) It has a skull marking?

ANSWERS ON PAGES 36–37

The **Answers** to Chapter One (PAGE 13)

1. Where would you find a Jacobson's organ?

Answer: b)

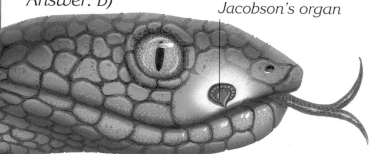

Jacobson's organ

A Jacobson's organ is a small pouch found in the mouths of amphibians and many **reptiles**, including snakes. It is lined with special cells that allow the animal to taste and smell the world around it. Tiny particles are carried from the ground, air, and water into the Jacobson's organ when it flicks its tongue in and out.

2. Which animal leaves a silvery trail?

Answer: a) and b)

Both slugs and snails produce a thick, slimy substance called mucus. It protects their bodies and helps them to glide over rough surfaces such as soil and the bricks of paths. It's easy to track snails and slugs because their mucus dries into a silvery trail.

3. Where can you find rods and cones?

Answer: b)

The eyes of **vertebrate** animals are lined with millions of tiny cells that react to light and help pass images to the brain. There are two kinds of cell in the lining of the eye, the retina. Rod cells can react in very dim light, but give only black-and-white vision. Cone cells detect color, but they need bright light.

HUMAN EYE

Iris

Cone

Rod

Day-active animal

Cone

Rod

Night-active animal

Pupil

Lens

Retina

Nocturnal animals are able to see in the dark because their eyes have many more rods than cones. Daytime animals have more cones than rods. As light enters the eye, it is focused by the lens. The iris controls the amount of light coming into the eye.

4. Who hangs upside down in dark caves?

Answer: c)

Many bats spend their days fast asleep—hanging upside down in caves, gripping onto rocky ledges with their hooklike claws. Some bats hibernate in their caves during cold winters—their temperature drops and they barely breathe as their bodies slow down into a deep, sleeplike state. The warmer weather in the spring makes them lively again.

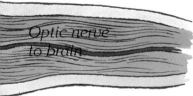

Optic nerve to brain

5. Which animal makes electricity to help it navigate?

Answer: b)

The electric knife fish is one of a few species of fish able to generate its own electricity to find its way in dark waters. It lives in murky rivers in South America. The large fin along its belly contains cells that give out weak amounts of electric light. (You can find out about glowworms on page 20.)

Fin

6. Which night animals send messages by drumming?

Answer: c)

Their long hind legs make gerbils look like a cross between a mouse and a kangaroo. They are often kept as pets, but in the wild they live in the deserts of Asia and Africa, coming out to feed in the cool of the night. Gerbils have sharp hearing and will warn of danger by drumming their feet.

7. Where are a cricket's ears?

Answer: c)

Yes, crickets really do listen with their legs! The tiny eardrum on the knee joint of each front leg can pick up very shrill sounds, such as the mating call of the males.

8. What is a Tasmanian devil?

Answer: b)

As its name suggests, the Tasmanian devil comes from the Australian island state of Tasmania. It is cat-sized, and a very fierce meat-eater that hunts at night. Tasmanian devils are marsupials, like koalas and kangaroos.

The **Answers** to Chapter Two (PAGE 21)

1. Which insects (other than moths) power dive to avoid bats?

Answer: b)
The giant lacewing (left) lives beside woodland streams, and spends the day resting beneath leaves. Fluttering on gauzy wings by night, it may be discovered by hungry bats. When attacked, the lacewing just folds its wings and drops like a stone to the ground.

2. Which insects can jam a bat's sonar?

Answer: c)
Some moths squeak back at attacking bats. This may confuse the bats' own echolocation signals, jamming their sonar. Or it may be a way of warning bats that these particular moths don't taste good.

3. Where do beetles keep their wings?

Answer: a)
The front wings of many beetles have developed into hard, protective cases called elytra (singular, elytron).

Elytron

The beetle's rear wings are used for flying and tuck neatly under the elytra when not in use. Ladybugs (above) are a kind of beetle. Their elytra are red, orange, or yellow, with black spots. The blood of ladybugs has a very nasty smell and taste, and predators soon learn to avoid these distinctively colored beetles. If attacked, a ladybug will squirt out some of its own blood in self-defense!

4. Which bird uses echolocation?

Answer: a)
Oilbirds (right) are ace fliers, and like many bats they use echolocation to fly around the dark caves where they live. The sounds given out by bats are usually too high for us to hear, but an oilbird's click-clacking is lower and sounds like a typewriter. When disturbed in their cave, oilbirds chatter and scream. (You can read about echolocation on pages 10 and 38.)

5. What's the difference between a bat and a bird?

Answer: a), b), and c)
Bats and birds belong to completely different groups of animals—flight is one of the few things they have in common. Birds have feathers and lay eggs. Bats are furry mammals and give birth to their young. A bat's wing is made from a thin layer of leathery skin, which is supported by the long finger bones of the bat's hand, almost like a tent on its frame.

6. Which of these isn't a vampire?

Answer: a), b), and c)
None of these animals is a bloodsucker. Oxpeckers and goatsuckers are a completely harmless species of bird. The false vampire bats (above) are large and look fierce, but they do not suck blood.

7. Which of these mammals can fly?

Answer: c)
Bats are the only mammals to have mastered flapping flight, but others can glide long distances between trees. The best glider is the colugo (left). It is wingless but can stretch out the flaps of skin between its limbs.

8. What is a nightjar?

Answer: b)
Nightjars are insect-eating nocturnal birds. The 67 species include the African pennant-winged nightjar (right), the whip-poorwill, and the European nightjar.

The **Answers** to Chapter Three (PAGE 31)

3. Which nocturnal animal were the ancient Romans particularly fond of?

Answer: a)

The Romans just loved edible dormice (below)—they ate them for dinner!

1. What is the owl monkey's other name?

Answer: a)

The douroucouli (above and page 27) is the only nocturnal monkey. It lives in Central and South American rain forests, where it eats fruit, insects, small birds, and mammals.

4. Which fish can breathe out of water?

Answer: a)

Most fish take life-giving oxygen from the water, but the walking catfish (below) can also take it from the air. This unusual fish crawls over sandbanks and dried-out riverbeds at night.

2. What do numbats and wombats have in common?

Answer: b)

Both of these night animals are Australian marsupials, like kangaroos and koalas. The numbat likes to lick up termites, while the burrowing wombat is a plant-eater.

5. Which nocturnal animal uses its middle finger like a fork?

Answer: c)

The aye-aye lives deep in the forests of Madagascar, an island off the coast of East Africa. It bites through tree bark with its sharp teeth, and then hooks out tasty grubs with its long, thin middle finger.

6. Which animal builds dams?

Answer: c)

There are two species of beaver—one lives in North America and the other in Europe. Beavers are strong swimmers and can stay under water for up to 15 minutes. They work hard after dark—felling trees with their front teeth, damming rivers with branches and mud, and building lodges (below).

7. Which marsupial sleeps in a tree all day long?

Answer: b)

Tree kangaroos (below) are dog-sized marsupials that live in Australian rain forests. They are rarely seen because they spend the day dozing in the branches. By night, they eat fruit and leaves.

8. How did the deathwatch beetle get its name?

Answer: b)

Deathwatch beetles attract mates in spring by knocking their heads against wood. Hearing this sound in old buildings at night led some people to believe that it was a warning of death!

USEFUL WORDS

AMPHIBIAN A member of a group of animals that includes frogs, toads, and newts. Most amphibians live part of their lives in water, and part on land. Their jellylike eggs are laid in water and develop into tadpoles.

CAMOUFLAGE A method of disguise. Many animals have built-in camouflage through body color, pattern, or shape. This helps them to blend in with their background and hide from predators.

CELL The smallest living unit. Animals and plants are built of cells. Some tiny life forms may be just one cell, but most animals are made up of millions.

COLONY A group of animals that live together in one place.

ECHOLOCATION Locating an object by the time taken for sounds to travel to it, and then bounce off and return (or echo). Many bats and some whales use echolocation to navigate and find food by sending out a stream of noise and listening to the echoes made as the sounds bounce off objects. Submarines use echolocation in their sonar equipment to find other craft, avoid obstacles, measure the depth of the water, and look for features on the seabed.

FUNGI Fungi (toadstools, mushrooms, and molds) are neither plant nor animal. Unlike plants, which are usually green and make their own food inside their bodies, fungi absorb ready-made food.

HIBERNATION A deep, sleeplike state that some animals enter when the weather is very cold or when food is scarce. The animals rarely wake and, instead of eating, they live off the fat stored in their bodies.

MAGNETIC FIELD A force pattern that surrounds a magnet (an object that attracts some metals, but particularly iron). The Earth is a huge natural magnet, with north and south magnetic poles.

MAMMAL A member of a group of animals that are warm-blooded and feed their young on milk made in the mother's breast. The group includes humans, cats, dogs, bats, bears, horses, cows, whales, wolves, and many other animals.

MARSUPIAL A member of a group of mammals whose young are born at a very early stage. They usually complete their development in a pouch on the mother's body.

MIGRATION The regular movement of animals to and from certain areas. Migration usually takes place at particular seasons of the year.

NECTAR A sweet, sugary solution produced by some flowers. It is the main food for many kinds of insect, some small birds, and a few other animals. Bees use nectar to make honey.

NOCTURNAL Living by night. Diurnal means living by day.

OXYGEN An invisible gas that makes up about one-fifth of the air around us. Almost all living things need oxygen to live. They use it to get energy from their food. Most land animals have lungs inside their bodies and take in oxygen from the air when they breathe. Most fish and some other water creatures have gills, which take oxygen from water. As water flows over the gills, oxygen passes from the water into the animal's blood (which flows inside the gills).

PLANKTON Tiny plants or animals that float in lakes or oceans. Most plankton are so small that they can only be seen under a microscope. Despite their size, they are a very important food source for fish and many other animals.

PREDATOR An animal that hunts and kills other animals for food.

PREY Animals that are hunted, killed, and eaten by other animals.

RAIN FOREST A kind of thick forest that grows mainly in tropical regions, but also in other areas with high rainfall.

REPTILE A member of a group of animals that includes snakes and lizards. Most reptiles have dry, scaly skin and their eggs have leathery shells.

SALIVA Another word for spit, the liquid produced in an animal's mouth.

SPECIES A species is an individual kind of plant or animal, such as a gorilla or a koala. All the members of a species look similar and can breed together.

TERRITORY The area of land marked out and defended by an animal for feeding or breeding.

TROPICAL A word used to describe the very hot lands near the equator, or animals that live in these regions.

VERTEBRATE An animal with a spine, or backbone. Fish, amphibians, reptiles, birds, and mammals are all vertebrates. Animals such as insects that do not have backbones are called invertebrates. There are around 45,000 known vertebrate species, and 1.2 million invertebrate species.

INDEX

albatross 23
amphibian 7, 24, 32, 38, 39
aye-aye 31, 37

badger 4, 28
barn owl 15
bat 10, 13, 14, 16–17, 19, 21,
  31, 33, 34, 35, 38
beaver 31, 37
bullfrog 24
bushbaby 27

camouflage 5, 15, 26, 38
cat 4, 10, 13, 26, 29, 38
catfish 25, 31, 36
cockroach 12, 13
colony 16, 27, 38
colugo 21, 35
crane fly 30
cricket 8, 13, 33

death's-head hawkmoth 18
deathwatch beetle 31, 37
dormouse 6, 31, 36
dwarf puff adder 5

earthworm 30
echolocation 10, 17, 19, 21,
  34, 35, 38
eel 7
electric knife fish 13, 33

false vampire bat 21, 35
fennec fox 11
firefly 20
fishing bat 17
flashlight fish 23
flying fox 16, 17
fox 4, 6, 28
frog 7, 8, 25, 29, 38
fruit bat 17
fungi 20, 38

gerbil 13, 33
giant lacewing 21, 34

glowworm 13, 20

hedgehog 29
hibernation 24, 33, 38
hippopotamus 25
howler monkey 9
hyena 29

jackrabbit 6
jellyfish 22

kakapo 15
kit fox 6
Kitti's hog-nosed bat 17
kiwi 12, 13

ladybug 34
lantern fish 23, 31
leaf-tailed gecko 5
lion 5
long-eared bat 10
loris 27

magnetic field 11, 38
mammal 16, 21, 25, 26, 27,
  35, 36, 38, 39
margay 26
marsupial 13, 31, 33, 36, 37,
  38
Mexican free-tailed bat 16
migration 11, 18, 39
mink 25
mole 30
moth 5, 6, 12, 13, 14, 18–19,
  21, 34
mouse 4, 15, 24, 28, 29, 31

nectar 6, 15, 17, 39
night heron 24
nightingale 9
nightjar 21, 35
numbat 31, 36

ocelot 26
oilbird 14, 21, 35

otter 22, 24, 25
owl 4, 9, 10, 14, 15, 27
owl monkey 27, 31, 36

pit viper 11
plankton 22, 23, 39
potto 26, 27, 31
predator 4, 5, 18, 19, 22, 24,
  28, 34, 38, 39
prey 6, 10, 11, 12, 15, 17, 25,
  26, 39

raccoon 29, 31
rain forest 9, 22, 26–27, 36,
  37, 39
rat 15, 29
reptile 32, 39
robber crab 5

salamander 7
scorpion 11, 15, 30
sea trout 25
shrew 30
slug 7, 13, 28, 30, 32
snake 5, 11, 12, 13, 27,
  32, 39
spider 11, 30
squid 22
storm petrel 23

tamandua 27
tarsier 27
Tasmanian devil 13, 33
tawny frogmouth 15
territory 8, 39
tiger 26
toad 8, 22, 24, 38
tree kangaroo 31, 37
tree pangolin 27

vampire bat 14, 16, 21, 35
vertebrate 32, 39

wolf 8, 16, 38
wombat 31, 36